VOCAL SELECTIONS from

D0117762

Cats is recorded on Geffen Records/Warner Bros. Records
PHOTOGRAPHY: Martha Swope

A Product Of
The Entertainment Company
40 WEST 57th STREET • NEW YORK, N.Y. 10019

Distributed by
HAL LEONARD PUBLISHING CORPORATION
Winona, MH 55987   Milwaukee, WI 53213

JELLICLE SONGS FOR JELLICLE CATS

Music by ANDREW LLOYD WEBBER
Text by TREVOR NUNN
and RICHARD STILGOE after T.S. ELIOT

Hal - le - lu - jah, an - gel - i - cal choir. ___

Not as Quick

The mys - ti - cal di - vin - i - ty of

un - a - shamed fe - lin - i - ty   Round   the   ca -

the - dral   rang   "Vi - vat."   Life   to   the

THE OLD GUMBIE CAT

Thoughtfully, in moderate time

Music by ANDREW LLOYD WEBBER
Text by T.S. ELIOT

BUSTOPHER JONES: THE CAT ABOUT TOWN

Music by ANDREW LLOYD WEBBER
Text by T.S. ELIOT

Dignified

OLD DEUTERONOMY

Music by ANDREW LLOYD WEBBER
Text by T.S. ELIOT

Slowly

I be-lieve it is Old Deu-ter-on-o-my well of all things;

Can it be real-ly! No, Yes, Ho! Hi! Oh my eye! _____ My mind may be wan-der-ing

but I con-fess, I be-lieve it is Old Deu-te-ro-no-my. _____

GUS: THE THEATRE CAT

Music by ANDREW LLOYD WEBBER
Text by T.S. ELIOT

Gracefully

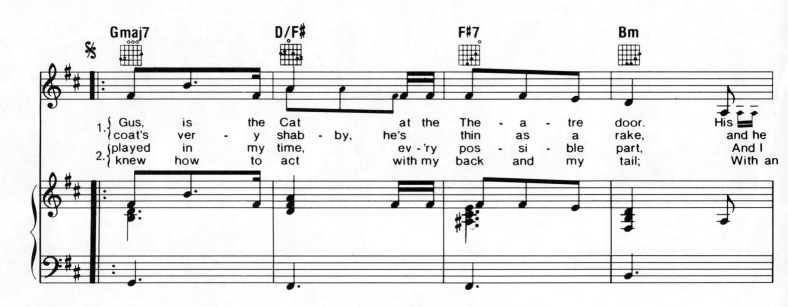

Gmaj7   D/F#   F#7   Bm

1. {Gus, is the Cat at the The-a-tre door.
   coat's ver-y shab-by, he's thin as a rake, His
2. {played in my time, ev-'ry pos-si-ble part, and he
   knew how to act with my back and my tail; With an

Em7   A   Dsus   D

name, as I ought to have told you be-fore, Is
suf-fers from pal-sy that makes his paw shake. Yet he
used to know sev-en-ty speech-es by heart. I'd ex-
hour of re-hear-sal, I nev-er could fail. I'd a

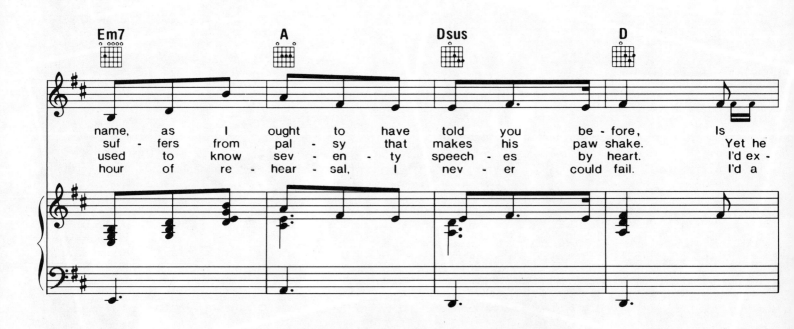

4th time To Coda

no-thing to e-qual, from what I hear tell; that mo-ment of

mys-ter-y when I made his-to-ry as Fire - frore-fid-dle the

Fiend of the Fell.

GUS (Sung reprise)

And I once crossed the stage on a telegraph wire
To rescue a child when a house was on fire
And I think that I still can much better than most
Produce blood-curdling noises to bring on the Ghost
I once played Growltiger, could do it again

SKIMBLESHANKS: THE RAILWAY CAT

Music by ANDREW LLOYD WEBBER
Text by T.S. ELIOT

MR. MISTOFFELEES

Tugger:

"You ought to know about Mr. Mistoffelees
the original Conjuring Cat. (There can be no
doubt about that.) Please listen to me and don't
scoff. All his inventions are off his own bat.
Theres no such cat in the Metropolis: He holds
all the patent monopolies, For performing
surprising illusions and creating eccentric confusions."

Music by ANDREW LLOYD WEBBER
Text by T.S. ELIOT

The great-est ma-gi -cians have some-thing to learn __ from

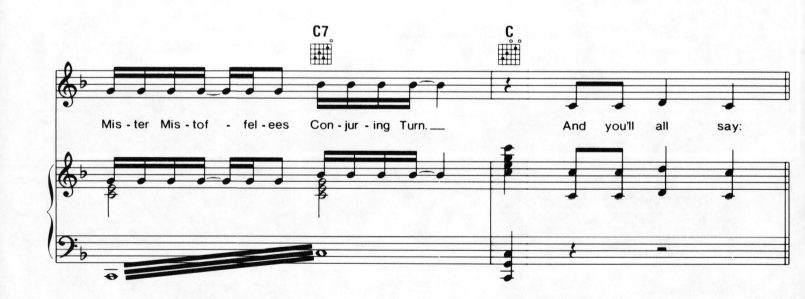

Mis-ter Mis-tof -fel-ees Con-jur-ing Turn. __ And you'll all say:

MEMORY

Music by ANDREW LLOYD WEBBER
Text by TREVOR NUNN after T.S. ELIOT

(alternate lyric)

MEMORY

Text by TREVOR NUNN
after T.S. ELIOT

DAYLIGHT, SEE THE DEW ON A SUNFLOWER
AND A ROSE THAT IS FADING
ROSES WITHER AWAY
LIKE THE SUNFLOWER I YEARN TO TURN MY FACE TO THE DAWN
I AM WAITING FOR THE DAY

MEMORY, TURN YOUR FACE TO THE MOONLIGHT
LET YOUR MEMORY LEAD YOU
OPEN UP, ENTER IN
IF YOU FIND THERE THE MEANING OF WHAT HAPPINESS IS
THEN A NEW LIFE WILL BEGIN

MEMORY, ALL ALONE IN THE MOONLIGHT
I CAN SMILE AT THE OLD DAYS
I WAS BEAUTIFUL THEN
I REMEMBER THE TIME I KNEW WHAT HAPPINESS WAS
LET THE MEMORY LIVE AGAIN

BURNT OUT ENDS OF SMOKEY DAYS
THE STALE COLD SMELL OF MORNING
THE STREELAMP DIES, ANOTHER NIGHT IS OVER
ANOTHER DAY IS DAWNING

DAYLIGHT, I MUST WAIT FOR THE SUNRISE
I MUST THINK OF A NEW LIFE
AND I MUSTN'T GIVE IN
WHEN THE DAWN COMES TONIGHT WILL BE A MEMORY TOO
AND A NEW DAY WILL BEGIN

SUNLIGHT, THROUGH THE TREES IN SUMMER
ENDLESS MASQUERADING
LIKE A FLOWER AS THE DAWN IS BREAKING
THE MEMORY IS FADING

TOUCH ME, IT'S SO EASY TO LEAVE ME
ALL ALONE WITH THE MEMORY
OF MY DAYS IN THE SUN
IF YOU TOUCH ME YOU'LL UNDERSTAND WHAT HAPPINESS IS
LOOK, A NEW DAY HAS BEGUN

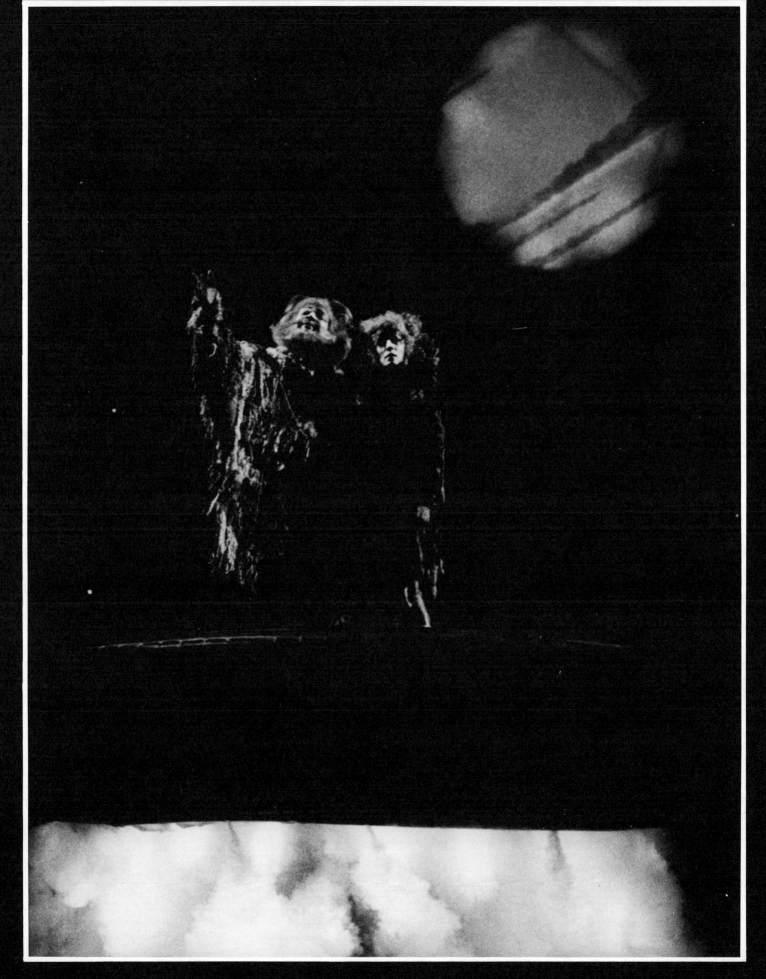

THE JOURNEY TO THE HEAVYSIDE LAYER

Music by ANDREW LLOYD WEBBER
Text by T.S. ELIOT

THE AD-DRESSING OF CATS

Music by ANDREW LLOYD WEBBER
Text by T.S. ELIOT